HIKING, RIDING & CYCLING THE POINT REYES TRAILS

Written by Dennis Portnoy

Copyright (c) 2018 by Dennis Portnoy. All rights reserved.
No part of this book may be reproduced, stored in a retrieval system or transmitted in any form or by any means, electronic, mechanical, photo copying, recording or otherwise without the prior permission of Dennis Portnoy. Please email inquiries to dennisportnoy@yahoo.com
ISBN is 9781726406963 and 1726406962

I have been riding, walking and cycling these trails for over twenty years. People often ask me for directions. Sometimes they want to know the fastest way back to the parking lot. They may ask the way to the beach or trails that avoid the hot sun.

The trails in Point Reyes are incredibly beautiful, varied with many miles of trails. You can enjoy the pine forests, see breathtaking ocean views and have access to beaches. There are over 150 miles of trails and roads and 70,000 acres of land. I wanted to make this guide as uncomplicated as possible. In order to accomplish this I organize the trails in two ways. First, I begin with the trails heading west, then the northern trails. I then describe the trails heading south, and east. Most of the trails begin at the Five Brooks Parking Lot.

For each trail I assign a number (1, 2 or 3) that indicates the degree of difficulty.
1 = the easiest in terms of steep hills and slippery conditions in the wetter months. 2= moderate and 3 is the most challenging. On the more narrow trails poison oak is a constantly changing situation, with some years being worse than other years.

I hope this guide makes your travels easier, more fun and safe.

Chapter one **WEST**

The BOLEMA-RIDGE-STEWARTS LOOP

Difficulty Scale 3

From the Five Brooks parking lot you go past the lake to the main trail *Stewarts* and take a left. Very soon you will turn right on the next trail called the *Olema Valley trail* heading south. Cyclist can ride on *Olema Valley* but not *Bolema*.

If you leave from Stewart's Camp you turn left on *Stewarts trail* toward the stables. Soon you will pass a road on your left but continue straight. You will see a trail on your right- turn right.

After ten minutes of being on a level trail, you start climbing up a narrow wooded trail and in a half hour it levels out.

You will come to a fork in the trail. Go right on *Bolema* heading west and up the steep trail for a half an hour.

(Continuing straight at this fork goes south to the *Texierra trail* and the southern and Eastern trail system)

When you reach the top of *Bolema* trail you have 3 trail choices:

1. You could turn left on the *Ridge trail* toward *Texierra* and or end up at *Palomarin*.
2. Continue straight *on Lake Ranch*.

For the purposes of doing the loop turn right on the *Ridge trail*, passing the *narrow Ridge trail* on your left, and intersecting with *Stewarts*, then turn right. (*)

This will wind down to the Five Brooks parking lot and to Stewarts Camp. (Turning left on Stewarts takes you west toward the beach.)

- If you went left onto the *narrow Ridge trail* in fifteen to thirty minutes you will exit at a different section of *Stewarts Trail*. Just before you reach *Stewarts trail* you will see a trail on your left that heads West called the *Alamea trail*. It goes to the *Old Out trail* and this will take you to the Coast trail.

When you reach *Stewarts trail* you could also go straight across to *Greenpicker*. Turning right will take you back to the Five Brooks parking lot. Veer left when you get to an intersection.

STEWARTS-RIDGE-BOLEMA Loop

Difficulty Scale 3

This is the same route we just described only in reverse. **From** *Stewarts Camp* or the Parking Lot you go right on *Stewarts trail*. In about an hour you will come to a fork in the road. Right is *Stewarts trail* headed toward the beach and left is the wider *Ridge trail*. Turn left on *Ridge* and go until you reach an intersection where three trails meet. Turn left at the *Bolema trail*.

(Straight/ South at this intersection goes to *Texierra, Palomarin*, and the *Coast trail*. Right takes you west on *Lake Ranch Trail* also ending at the *Coast trail*.)

The *Bolema trail* is steep and narrow, and as you go down hill it ends at the *Olema Valley trail*. Turning left on *Olema Valley* and in twenty minutes to a half-hour you will be back to the beginning of Stewarts trail and the Parking Lot.

Turning right at *Olema valley* takes you to the Southern trail system.

THE LAKE RANCH TRAIL TO THE COAST TRAIL

Difficulty Scale 2

At the top of the *Bolema trail* coming up from the *Olema Valley trail* is the *Ridge trail* and *Lake Ranch* is straight ahead. You can also get to *Lake Ranch* by heading up *Stewarts* then turning left at the *Ridge Trail*.

Continuing on *Lake Ranch* it is about six miles to the *Coast trail*. When you reach the *Coast trail* turning right will take you north toward Bass Lake, *Old Out trail*, and Wildcat Beach. Turning left takes you to *Palamarin parking lot*.

Continuing down *Lake Ranch* right before Mudd Lake (which is really a pond) there is a horse hitch on your right. The trail widens and is surrounded by woods. Fifteen to thirty minutes after passing Mudd Lake there is a lot of poison oak on both sides of the trail.

You will pass a trail on your right called *Crystal Lake trail* that has not been maintained and is loaded with poison oak. (This trail goes directly to the *Coast trail* and exits near Bass Lake. At the time this book is being written the trail is closed and impassable. It may open again some day.)

You can return to the Five Brooks lot by retracing your steps or by taking *Old Out* to *Stewarts* trail.

STEWARTS TRAIL

Difficulty Scale 3

The *Stewart's Trail* is the main artery and a wide trail that is open to hikers, cyclists and horses. The National Park vehicles drive to Wildcat and Glen Camp. From the Five Brooks parking lot you go past the pond then turn right. *Stewart's Trail* ascends and goes east to west seven miles to Wildcat Beach.

The last two miles down to the beach are a steep downhill grade with beautiful views.

As you head west there are several trails that branch out from Stewart's. The first is *Greenpicker* off to your right about a mile up the road. About an hour from the parking lot on your left is the *wider Ridge Trail*. Continuing on Stewart's Trail to the beach you will see a *narrow Ridge trail* on your left. Further down the road on your left is *Old Out Trail*. Another few miles and *Glen Trail* is on your right. Then, you will see the *Coast Trail* on the right.

STEWARTS TRAIL OFFSHOOTS
1) GREENPICKER TRAILS

Greenpicker is a six-mile long trail that goes west and east beginning at *Stewarts trail* and ending at *Glen trail*. For hikers who are camping at Glen Camp it is the quickest route, and there are no vehicles or bicycles.

The trail begins a half-mile up the *Stewarts trail* from the Five Brooks parking lot. You will see a narrow trail on your right. This first section is a 3 on the difficulty scale. You climb for over a mile on the steep narrow trail and then it levels out and widens. This is a lovely section to canter your horse. It is about a quarter mile and level with woods on both sides of you. Toward the end of the level part on your right is a continuation of *Greenpicker*. A sign reads "Glen trail 1.4". **Veer right**.

If you don't go right but stay straight for five minutes you will be back on *Stewarts trail*. There is a small sign on Stewarts that reads FIR TOP.

A little secret: If you exit where *Greenpicker* FIRST intersects with the *Stewarts trail* at Fir Top go right on *Stewarts Trail*. About thirty yards on your left you will see a driveway. It is a very short distance to a meadow with two horse hitches. It is a good place to eat, or rest.

If you continue right for fifteen minutes **on the *Stewarts trail*** toward the ocean you will reach an intersection. *Narrow Ridge trail* is on your left and if you took that right very soon you will be back on *Greenpicker*. The *narrow Ridge trail* on your left is a mile long trail (1 on the difficulty scale) connecting with the *wider Ridge trail*. From here you are ten to twenty minutes from the *Bolema Trail* and *Lake Ranch trail*.

If you veer right from *Stewarts* you will see *Greenpicker*. Right takes you back to the Five Brooks parking lot. Left on *Greenpicker* heads west toward the *Glen Trail*. This section of *Greenpicker* is a 1 on the difficulty scale.

If you were to continue straight on *Stewarts* and not turn left on *narrow Ridge* or right to *Greenpicker* in a quarter of a mile you will see *Old Out trail* on your left.
When you were heading west and where you veered right after the level part of *Greenpicker,* in a mile you will see a trail off to your left.

If you are heading south on *Greenpicker* the trail will split and on your right is a sign that reads:

Greenpicker Trail
Glen Camp 1.7
Glen Trail 1.0
Wildcat Camp 2.8
Fir Top 0.4
Five Brooks 3.6

9

If you took that left very soon you will exit at another section of the *Stewarts trail*. Directly in front of you heading south toward *Alamea* and *Bolema* is the narrow part of the *Ridge trail*. Left on *Stewarts trail* takes you back toward Five Brooks Parking Lot. Right goes to Wildcat.

Continue straight on *Greenpicker* going west and it ends at the *Glen Trail*. It is 1 on the difficulty scale. You will be on gentle hills and level sections.
Right on *Glen Trail* is the quickest way to Glen Camp, Millers Point and to access the Northern trails.

Turning right on *Glen* takes you to Glen Camp in a half a mile. Left on *Glen* takes you back to *Stewarts trail* in less then a mile.

Pretty soon on your right you will see *Glen Spur north* that goes to Millers point, and *Glen Spur south* that dead ends at the *Coast trail*. Left at *Coast* is one way to get to Wildcat, and it is a 2 on the difficulty scale. Right takes you to Millers Point, and is a 1 on the difficulty scale.

In the rainy season *Greenpicker* can be very slippery.

2) THE RIDGE TRAIL

Difficulty scale 2

I mention the *Ridge Trail* because, aside from it facing South and North and the southern trails system, it connects you to *Bolema, Little* Ridge and *Lake Ranch* (which head West).

Turning left off of *Stewarts trail* going south on the *Ridge trail* is seven miles to the Palomarin parking lot. Entering the Ridge trail from Stewart's is a short distance to the *narrow Ridge trail* on your right.

It is a mile from Stewarts trail to where *Bolema* and *Lake Ranch* intersect. It also is three miles to *Texierra trail* that runs East and West.

3) THE LITTLE RIDGE TRAIL

1 on the difficulty scale

When you are heading west on *Stewart's trail* after about three miles the hill flattens out and there is a small meadow on your right. A narrow trail to your right quickly connects with *Greenpicker trail*.

You continue downhill on *Stewarts* and in less than a half-mile there are two narrow trails on your right and left. The trail on your right joins *Greenpicker trail*. The one on your left is the *narrow Ridge trail*. It is a mile long and it crosses *Alamea trail* on your right and ends at the *wider Ridge trail*.

4) OLD OUT TRAIL

Difficulty scale 2

If you continue on *Stewart's* after passing the *narrow Ridge Trail* it becomes a steep decent, and in a quarter of a mile you will see *Old Out Trail* on your left.

Old Out begins as a narrow trail then widens. It passes the *Alamea trail* on the left, and it is about three miles from *Stewart's trail* to the Coast trail.

As you head down to the coast in the summer and fall watch for poison oak crossing the trail.

When you reach the *Coast trail* turning left takes you to Bass Lake and to the *Lake Ranch trail* in about two miles. If you turn right in less then one mile you will reach Wildcat Beach.

5) COAST TRAIL

Difficulty Scale 2

If you go on this section of the *Coast trail* from *Stewarts trail* you will be heading north toward Millers Point, Glen Camp and the Northern trail system. You can also access *Greenpicker* and return to the Five Brooks parking lot. It is a gradual climb with great ocean views.

It levels out at the top and there are moments where you see hills on your right then you become surrounded with Pine trees.

After about a mile you can turn right at the *Glen Spur South trail* to get to the *Glen trail* or continue straight to Millers Point and Arch Rock. From *Stewarts Trail* to *Bear Valley road is* 3.0 miles.

WILDCAT CAMP and BEACH

Wildcat Camp nestled into the hills and is very close to the beach. There is a toilet, horse hitch, water trough, a water fountain, a bike rack, camping sites and picnic tables.

You may see a few tents depending on the time of year. The beach is about a half-mile long and at the end there is a waterfall.

Sometimes the entrance to the beach can be steep, narrow and challenging for horses.

There are three ways to get to Wildcat Beach from the Five Brooks parking lot:

You can follow *Stewarts trail* all the way to the end.

You can take *Lake Ranch* beginning from the top of *Bolema*, then go right at the *Coast trail*.

Or, **from** *Stewarts trail* you can turn left at *Old Out*, then turn right at the *Coast trail* and ride for fifteen minutes to the beach.

RETURNING to five Brooks parking lot FROM Wildcat Beach

You can take the *Coast trail* from *Wildcat* South toward Bass Lake, pass *Old Out* and go left at *Lake Ranch*, (three miles) then follow it six miles till you reach *Ridge trail*. At this juncture you will go straight down *Bolema,* then left on *Olema.*

(If you don't turn left the *coast trail* dead ends in three miles at the Palomarin parking lot). Wildcat to Palomarin can get crowded with hikers on weekends.) *Palamarin Trail* is a 1 on the difficulty scale but after the rains it can be a 2.

OR

From Wildcat you could take the *Coast trail* to the *Old Out trail*, turn left until you reach *Alamea* or *Stewarts trail*, and then turn right.

You can also take the *Stewarts trail* all the way home or where *Stewarts* intersects with to the narrow *Ridge* trail–then turn right on the wider *Ridge*, then left on *Bolema*, and another left on *Olema.*

Alamea is 2 on the difficulty scale and is about a mile long ending at the narrow *Ridge Trail*. You could go left to *Stewart's* or right to the wider *Ridge Trail* then go left on *Bolema* then left on the *Olema Valley* trail.

When you are on this section of the *Coast Trail* heading south to *Lake Ranch* from December to July poison oak branches can swipe your limbs. The trail crew usually comes in July to widen the trail.

Once you leave *Wildcat* and take the *Coast trail* south toward *Lake Ranch* you will pass two lakes on your right. In certain times of the year in the morning Pelican Lake sounds like a symphony.

This section of the *Coast trail* is narrow and has both level and some hilly spots. At times you are high up and overlooking the expansive coast and spectacular views.

When riding the *Coast trail* **from** Wildcat or from *Old Out* toward *Lake Ranch trail* (about three quarters of the way to *Lake Ranch*) on your right is Bass Lake.

When you head south from Wildcat just b*efore* you reach the *Old Out trail* you will see a trail on your right that says *Ocean Lake Loop*. This trail parallels the *Coast trail* and detours for 0.8 miles ending up back on *Coast trail*.

There are nice views of the ocean and it gets narrow with steep high cliffs. If you are on a horse only take this trail if it is dry and your horse has good footing and doesn't spook.

Continuing to ride toward *Lake Ranch trail* watch for poison oak on both sides and branches possibly crossing the trail.

COAST TRAIL:
PALOMARIN TO WILDCAT

The southern entrance to the Park is the quickest way to get to Bass Lake and Alamere Falls at Wildcat Beach. When you are on Highway 1 take the turn off to Bolinas and drive toward the ocean on Mesa Road. At some point it becomes a dirt road that goes a few miles and dead ends at a Parking Lot. The Lot can get quite crowded on a weekend in the warm months. The trail begins at the Parking Lot and heads north about 3 miles to Bass Lake, then another 2 1/2 miles to Alamere Falls.

From the Palomarin Lot, in about a half hour you will see the *Lake Ranch* trail on your right (east). It is seven miles and takes you to the Five Brooks Lot. **People frequently turn here and get lost.**

Once you pass *Lake Ranch* <u>continue straight</u> on the *Coast trail* and you will see the large lake on your left. You will see a tiny stream and a small water trough on your right.

If you are traveling south **from** Wildcat you will pass two lakes on your right, neither of which you can access. On the weekends and in the warmer months the *Coast trail* can be busy with hikers and some horses. Bass Lake can be crowded and there is no horse access to the lake, but there are hitches up a short hill from the open area. People can walk down a short steep trail and take a dip.

THE RIDGE -ALEMEA-OLD OUT LOOP

Difficulty Scale 1

It would be too confusing to introduce this trail before you understood the continuing *Stewarts trail* west, *Old Out* and *Greenpicker*.

This is a great loop. When you leave from Stewarts Camp or the Five Brooks parking lot it is mainly uphill and the return is downhill. *Alamea trail* is a narrow half-hour trail surrounded by woods. It goes East and West from the narrow section of *Ridge trail* to the *Old Out trail*.

There are two ways of doing this loop.

One way is to go up *Stewarts* passing FIR TOP, go left on *Old Out*, than another left on *Alamea* and this will intersect with the *narrow Ridge trail*.

You can go right to the *big Ridge Trail* and left at *Bolema* then *Olema*.

The other way is when you get on the *narrow part of Ridge from Stewarts* or *Greenpicker*. You can take a right at *Alamea* to *Old Out* and you go Right to *Stewarts* and head back toward the Five Brooks parking lot. There are no bikes allowed on *Old Out* or *Alamea*.

MILLERS POINT

Miller's Point was named after Clem Miller, a Congressman for the district who in the nineteen sixties fought to protect the National Park from developers wanting to build for commercial use.

Millers Point overlooks the ocean and offers expansive views of Point Reyes where it juts out toward the Lighthouse. On a clear day you can see the Farralon Islands. It is on the *Coast trail* and you could continue North down a steep hill to get to Arch Rock, *Bear valley Road* and the Northern trail system.

Millers point is only a mile and a half from Glen Camp.

There are several ways to get to Millers Point from the Five Brooks parking lot or from Stewarts Camp. You can take *Stewarts trail* west and in six miles turn right at the *Coast trail*. You climb up the *Coast trail* one mile and continue straight after passing two narrow trails on your right; the first one is a short ride to the *Glen trail*.

The next narrow trail will take you to the *Glen trail* and, if you veer left, it goes to Glen Camp *.

After you pass the second trail Millers Point is about a quarter mile on your left. You will see a clearing and two large rocks.

22

Another way to get to Millers Point is to go west on *Greenpicker trail* until it ends at the *Glen trail.* (Turning right at the *Glen trail* takes you to *Glen Camp*). You will, instead, go left on *Glen* for a short while and will see a narrow trail on your right that has a sign that reads "Bear Valley 1.4".

You will get to fork in the trail. **Go left on *Glen Spur north*.** (If you were to go straight it goes to Glen Camp. You will reach another fork and right is 0.9 miles to Glen Camp.

Straight or north takes you to Bear valley Road in about two miles.)

Glen Spur North will soon end at the *Coast trail* where you turn right and in a quarter of a mile will see Millers Point.

Another alternative route is to go west on *Stewarts trail* for five miles till you see the *Glen Trail*, make a right and turn left at either of the two narrow trails that are on your left. They both take you to the *Coast trail* where you will go right.

Glen Camp is about three miles from Wildcat Camp. From Glen Camp you can take the *Coast trail* via Millers Point to *Stewarts* then turn right.
You can **return** to the Five Brooks parking lot from Millers Point by taking the *Glen trail* and going back south to *Stewarts trail* then turning left, or you can take *Greenpicker* back.

You could also get back to the Five Brooks parking lot by going east on *Greenpicker* to the first intersection, then turn right for a very short time and then head straight on the *narrow Ridge trail* till it dead ends at the *wider Ridge trail*. From here you could turn left to *Stewarts trail* or go right to *Bolema* then left at *Olema Valley trail*. Glen Camp is a small campground that has water, a bathroom, a few campsites and several picnic tables.

HORSES, HIKERS AND CYCLISTS

I have been fortunate to be a hiker, cyclist and equestrian. There have been situations where people have ended up getting hurt on the trails. The vast majority of cyclists are responsible and considerate. There is, however, a minority of cyclists whose goal is to go as fast as possible, even on narrow trails where bikes are prohibited.

Most cyclists and hikers have good intentions, but simply don't understand horses. Here are a few tips to keep in mind when you cross paths with them:

- Similarly to humans, horses each have their own unique personality and temperament. Some are more tolerant of sudden movements and sounds than others.

- Groups who are on a trail ride are often not experienced and don't have the skills to contain a scared animal.

- Even more experienced riders may not have learned to manage their horse's scared behavior.

   * When you approach a horse on your bike from behind or head on, *slow down*! Let the rider and the horse hear your friendly reassuring voice.

   * From a distance a horse may not recognize that you are a human, but sees instead shadows or movements. It may not be clear whether you are a person or a mountain lion. Again, your reassuring voice really helps.

- If you are walking on a narrow trail with a large backpack allow horses to pass, and have your pack facing away from them.

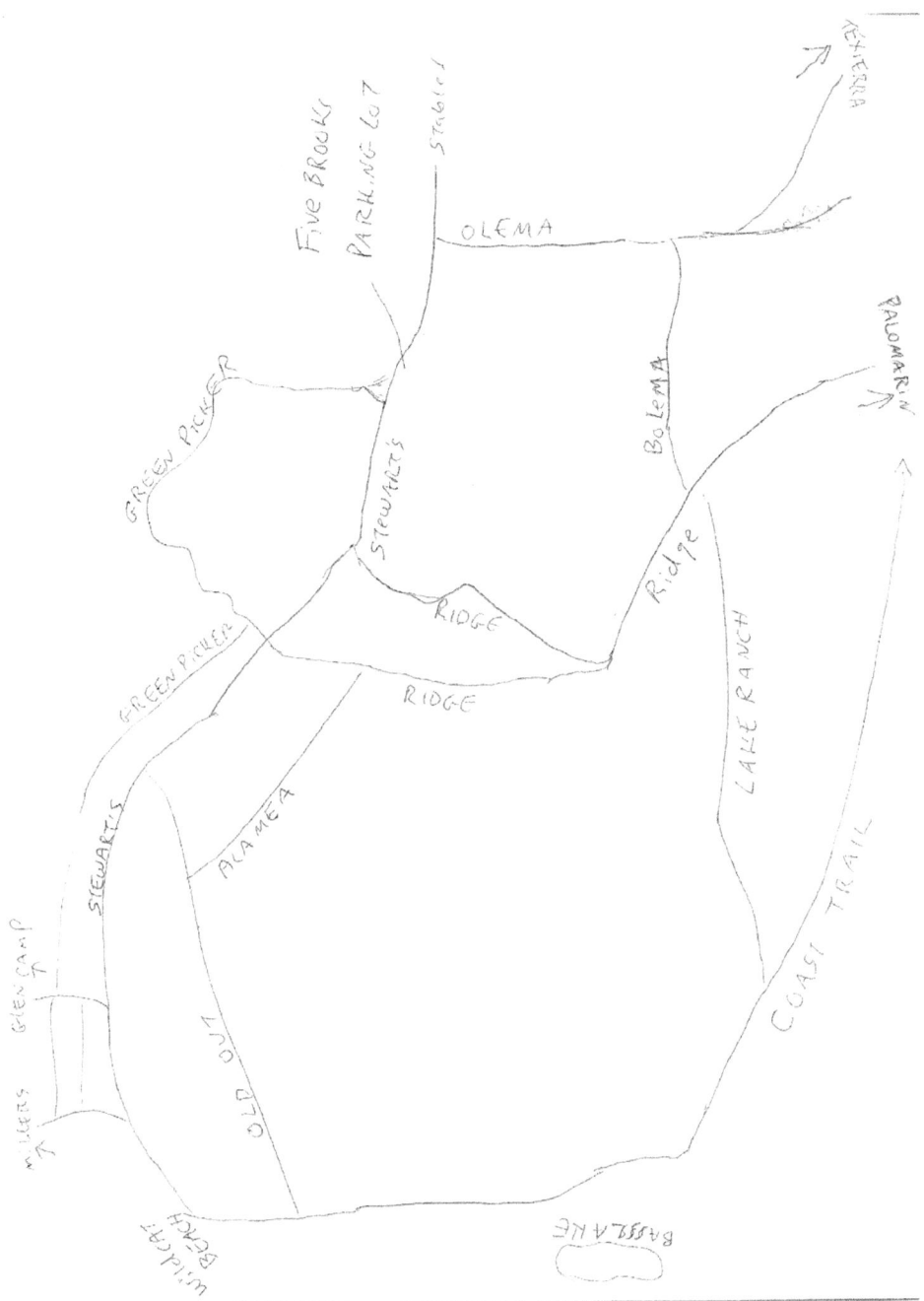

CHAPTER TWO   NORTH

RIFT ZONE

Difficulty Scale 1

When you are heading to the *Rift Zone trail* there is a short cut from the parking lot that goes to Stewarts Camp. It is very soon and across from the lake and on the right when you leave the parking lot. We don't usually go this route because there may be poison oak crossing the trail or people and horses at the base, and the horses can get startled.

The Rift Zone trail from the Five Brooks parking lot to the Vedanta cow meadow is four miles.

After you leave the Five Brooks parking lot you will see *Stewarts trail* and go right. About five hundred feet on your right is a gate. Go around the gate and head downhill. You will be entering Stewarts Camp. It may be crowded with horses and trailers between May and October (particularly on weekends).

Ride through the camp on the trail heading south to the small creek. Cross the creek and stay on the trail. The next quarter of a mile of the trail can be wet and slippery in the winter and in the spring.

You will cross a wooden bridge. The trail is narrow and is a minor climb. You will enter the property of the Vedanta Retreat.

Then the trail widens and there are trees and fences on both sides. Sometimes you may run into a few cows. It is a gradual downhill.

You will then enter the Vedanta religious retreat center. *Rift Zone* trail is on the San Andreas Fault. On your right you will see a green marshy pond. The ground opened up here in the 1908 earthquake and created a hole that is now filled with water.

About a half-mile further at the bottom of the hill you take a hard right and go about thirty feet to a green gate. Open it and stay on that trail. It widens and you will be heading into a wide cow pasture. Right after going through the gate you will pass cow paddocks on your right with no cows inside.

In about ten minutes you will see a water trough for the cows and a few large trees so there may be several cows hanging around near the entrance.

Continuing north through the pasture, and you reach the driveway to the Vedanta retreat driveway and another gate. Turning right on the driveway takes you to Highway One. If you go left on the Highway One in a quarter of a mile there is a restaurant. In the rear are hitches for horses.

Continue straight through yet another gate and a field. It is a half- mile to the Bear Valley Visitors center and parking lot. Once you go over a wooden bridge you will be on National Park property.

On your right is a parking lot and if you cross *Bear Valley Road* and continue straight a trail goes to the Morgan Ranch. (The Bear Valley road is *closed to horses on weekends* but there are many trails right near the parking lot that are available on the weekend).

I have been talking about beginning your trek at the Five Brooks Parking lot. You can also enter and exit the northern trails using Bear Valley Road. If you are camping at Glen Camp it may be easier for you.

BEAR VALLEY ROAD

Difficulty Scale 1

If you go left on *Bear Valley Road* **coming from** *Rift Zone* it's almost four miles to the *Coast trail* and Arch Rock *. As you continue on Bear Valley toward the Coast there are several offshoot trails on your right that are a mile long and head north.

The first is the *Wittenberg trail*. Then, the *Meadow trail* climbs up to Mt. Wittenberg (nice views), the *Sky trail* and Sky Camp.

Continuing on Bear valley Road the next trail is the *Old Pine trail* and you will see bathrooms on your right. In another fifteen minutes you will come to *Baldy trail* where you will see a bike rack. It is 3.2 miles from the Bear Valley parking lot to the bike rack.

(*Glen Trail* is on your left directly across from *Baldy* and it goes south toward Glen Camp and Millers Point. When climbing Glen trail you will reach a fork in the trail-left goes to Glen Camp. Right goes to Millers Point.)

You will reach a fork in the road. Turning right at the fork soon takes you on the *Coast trail*, paralleling the ocean and heading north several miles to Coast Camp. This section of the *Coast trail* goes several miles to Limantour beach. On the way is Sculptured Beach.

Left goes to five minutes to Arch Rock. Right before getting to Arch Rock there is a narrow trail on your left that goes left through the woods.

If you took this left it goes over a bridge and is a steep half-mile climb back to Millers Point with beautiful views of the ocean.

(CAUTION: Arch Rock is too dangerous for horses).

* Arch Rock is a large rock that juts out into the sea, and can accommodate several people for viewing.

CROSSING BEAR VALLEY FROM RIFT ZONE

From the Five Brooks parking lot going north on *Rift Zone* you cross Bear Valley road, go straight and around the Morgan Ranch.

After you pass the Morgan Ranch you will see a trail called *Kule Loklo* on your right. Stay straight and you will see a bridge and another trail called *Olema Marsh* that goes off to the right. This trail passes by the Indian Village.

If you don't take *Kule Koklo* and continue straight and go over the bridge, this is where *Horse trail* begins. *Horse trail* is a gradual climb that has a few level areas. At the top there's a trail on your left called *Z Ranch*. Do NOT turn on *Z Ranch* but continue straight, and in ten-twenty minutes you will turn left on a wider trail that goes to Sky Camp.

At Sky camp there are picnic tables, campsites, a water trough, bathrooms, a water fountain and beautiful views of the ocean.

KULE LOKLO INDIAN VILLAGE
Difficulty Scale 1

After passing the Morgan Ranch you will turn right when you come to the first trail. It is 0.2 miles to the village. You will pass a picnic area and ride on a gradual downhill past storage buildings.

With eucalyptus and pine trees on both sides soon there is a sign for the village where you turn left. On this trail you will come across a small village with a tepee, dance house and sweat lodge commemorating the Coast Miwok Indians. After the village if you continue straight for ten minutes the trail will fork. Left goes to the Highway for cars only and right is the *Olema Marsh* trail.

If you go right on *Olema Marsh* you will parallel Sir Francis Drake paved Road. It is a level trail that has some open views. The trail goes for one-mile and ends at the paved road. (There is a large sign that says "WHOA". The road goes to the town of Point Reyes, but can be dangerous because of the traffic and cars.)

To get back heading to the Five Brooks parking lot you need to turn around on *Olema Marsh*. You then turn left onto *Horsetrail*, cross Bear Valley Road, and continue straight on *Rift Zone*.

OTHER WAYS TO GET TO SKY CAMP

You can also get to Sky Camp by taking the *Baldy trail* or *Old Pine trail* from Bear Valley Road. Turning right on *Sky trail* takes you to Sky Camp.

Another option is to head up *Horse trail* from Bear Valley Road and at *Z Ranch* trail and turn left (west). Soon you will connect with Mt Wittenberg that intersects with *Sky trail*. Go right on *Sky trail* to Sky Camp.

Staying straight on *Sky trail* goes toward the ocean. (When you are on *Z Ranch trail* you will reach the base of Mt Wittenberg. A sharp left takes you on the *Meadow trail* back to Bear Valley. This option is available for horses on weekdays only.)

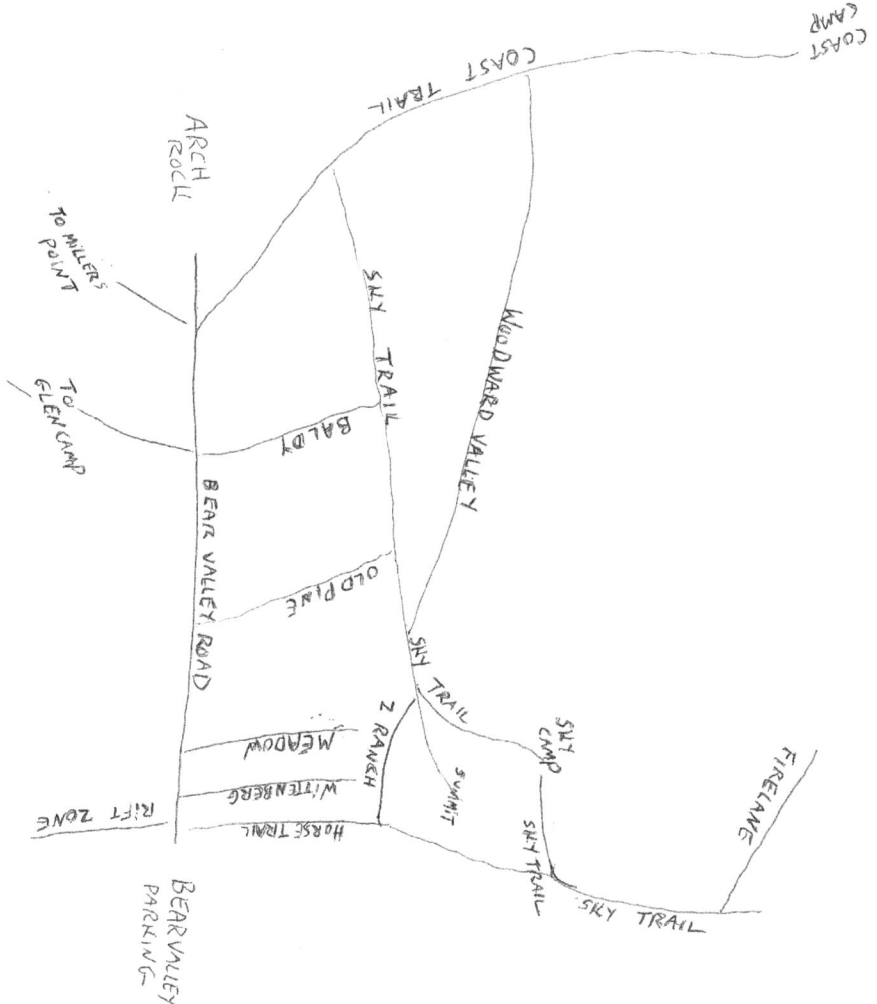

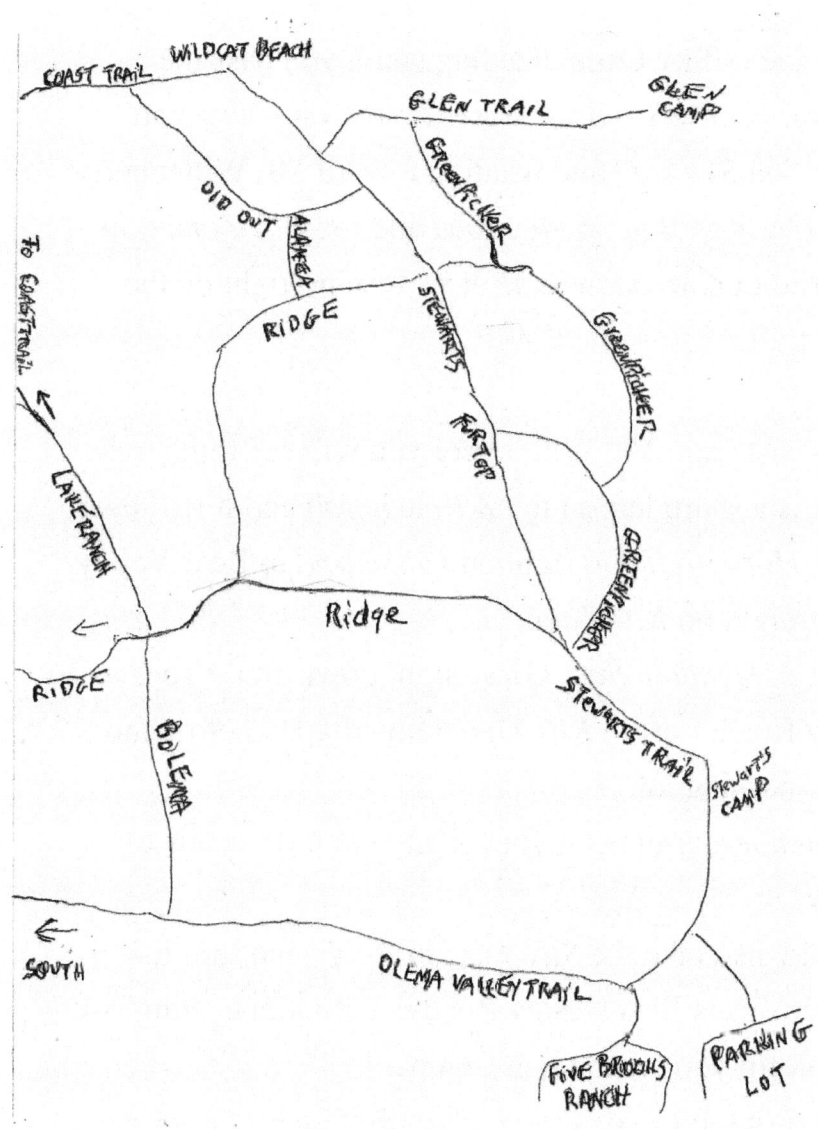

RETURNING to Five brooks FROM SKY CAMP

When you exit Sky Camp heading south you pass the bathrooms on your left and the water trough on your right. You are now on *Sky trail* and heading toward Mt. Wittenberg. You can get back to *Bear Valley road* and the *Rift Zone* trail by turning right on *Meadow trail* or by turning right on the *Wittenberg* trail.

Heading east from Mt. Wittenberg you will see three trails.

The first is a sharp left on the *Z Ranch trail* and it will take you back to *Horse trail*. Go right on *Horse trail* to Bear Valley Road and straight on *Rift Zone*.

The next is *Meadow trail*. Go straight down and it goes to Bear Valley Road. Left to *Rift Zone* immediately before the Bear Valley parking lot.

The *Wittenberg trail* is on your right, and it descends to Bear Valley.

You could also take the *Sky Trail* to *Baldy* and turn left. Where *Baldy* meets Bear Valley Road you continue straight on the *Glen trail* till you reach Glen Camp.

You will turn left on to *Greenpicker* till it ends at *Stewarts trail*. You could also take *Greenpicker* to the first intersection and cross *Stewarts,* continuing straight on the narrow part of the *Ridge trail* that takes you to the wider section of the *Ridge trail*.

Once you reach the *wider Ridge trail* you can turn left to *Stewarts trail* or right to the *Bolema trail*. This is also the fastest way home if you are at Glen Camp or Millers Point.

SKY TRAIL

Difficulty Scale 2

The *Sky trail* has Douglas Fur trees, Huckleberry and Wild Rose. It is a 5.6 mile-long and narrow trail that goes east to west from Limantour Road to *the Coast trail*. Several trails intersect with the *Sky trail*.

Traveling west from Mt. Wittenberg on the *Sky trail* you will see *Woodward Valley trail* on your right. This trail goes to the coast, is 2.7 miles long and is curvy, narrow and quite steep. It could take over an hour to get to Coast Camp by horse.

If you continue west on *Sky* on your left is *Baldy* trail. It is 2.4 miles long. It takes you to Bear Valley Road and you can take the *Glen Trail* if you want to head south. It is four miles from Sky Camp to the *Baldy trail*.

If you are on *Baldy* coming from the *Sky trail* you turn right on the Bear Valley Road if you want to go west toward the coast.

After you pass *Baldy* you will reach *Old Pine trail* on your left, and it is 1.9 miles to *Bear Valley road*. It is narrow, shady in the pines and is the least steep route to and **from** *Bear Valley road* to the *Sky trail*.

If you continue straight on the *Sky trail* it goes to the Coast. You will exit at the *Coast trail* and you will be a half hour north of Arch Rock.

If you are heading northeast from Sky Camp *the Sky trail* goes a quarter of a mile and the road ends. You are still on *Sky* but heading north and south. Turning right will take you back to *Horse trail* toward Bear Valley. If you go left very soon you will see *Firelane trail*. It is a narrow wooded trail that descends to Coast Camp 3.3 miles.

The Youth Hostel and the Environmental center are 3.2 miles. *Laguna trail* intersects in .7 miles. Pass the *Firelane trail* and very soon the road ends at Limantour Road.

FIRELANE TRAIL TO COAST CAMP

Difficulty Scale 3

Coming from Bear Valley on *Horse trail* facing north you pass *Z Ranch* trail on your left and the next left goes to Sky Camp. Don't turn left –stay straight and you will see *Firelane trail* on your left.

The sign reads 3.3 miles to Coast Camp and 2.2 miles to the *Laguna trail*.

Firelane is a narrow trail in the Pines with some wonderful ocean views. It begins fairly level and gradually descends. Heading toward the coast you reach the fork in the road where you can go left *on Laguna* to Coast Camp or right to the Youth hostel. If you go right for few miles you will see a private home and it intersects with the western section of the *Bayview trail*.

There is a small parking lot and a street that doesn't have much traffic. Turn left at the street and it's ten to twenty minutes to the Youth Hostel. Five minutes further is the southern entrance to the *Coast trail*.

(If you don't turn left on the *Coast trail* and, instead go straight through the intersection on the street you will reach another entrance to the *Bayview trail* and the *Muddy Hollow* trail in 0.4 miles.)

This section of the *Coast trail* is wide and level. You will be heading north back in the direction where you began and it is 1.5 miles to Limantour Beach, then another 1.4 miles to Coast Camp. When you get to the beach you can ride your horse on the sand to Coast Camp or stay on the main trail.

LAGUNA TRAIL

Difficulty Scale 2

If you continue north from that parking lot on Limantour road, you will be on a narrow trail that parallels the paved road and goes for a quarter of a mile. This is *Bayview trail*. The trail reaches Limantour road again and continues once you cross the paved road.

Just before you cross you will see the *Laguna trail* on your left. *Laguna* travels west toward the ocean and is a narrow, wooded trail that is level at first then gently declines. There are some nice ocean views.

You will see a few buildings and this is the Environmental Center. At this point you will be close to the Youth Hostel.

On your left is a little short trail that dead ends called *Hidden Valley*. Continue straight and go over the bridge and in a mile of a slight climb you will intersect with *Firelane* trail on your left.

Continuing straight on *Laguna* takes you to the *Coast trail*. *Firelane* will take you are back at the *Sky trail*.

You can get to Limantour Beach and Coast Camp via *Laguna* or the *Firelane trail*.

At the Environmental Center parking lot is another trail head for the *Laguna trail*.

BAYVIEW TRAIL (*No bikes*)
Difficulty Scale 1

Once you cross the paved road you will see another parking area. You can trailer your horse to this lot and begin your ride here. There are two trails that begin here. Left is *Bayview* and straight is *Inverness Ridge trail*.

It can take forty-five minutes to an hour from Sky Camp to this parking lot. *Bayview* is about 4-5 feet wide and fairly level. It can get crowded with hikers on hot weekends. You will get some nice glances of ocean views.

Bayview trail goes 2.8 miles northwest toward Muddy Hollow. From the parking lot it is 1.8 miles to *Muddy Hollow road*. There are some nice views, and it is about an hour to *Drakes View trail*. It is your first right and it goes east 1.8 miles and connects with another section of the *Inverness Ridge trail*.

Continuing straight on *Bayview*, crossing the bridge the road widens and you will reach an intersection where you can go left or right. This wider trail is *Muddy Hollow Road*. Left takes you to the *Muddy Hollow trail*. Right goes to the *Glenbrook trail* and this is one way to access the *Estero trail*.

On your way to *Glenbrook* on your first right is *Drakes view trail* and your next right is the western trailhead for the *Bucklin trail*.

Bucklin (a 3 on the difficulty scale) climbs to the *Inverness Ridge trail* (2 on the difficulty scale) where you can then go left to Mt. Vision or right takes you back to the Bayview Parking lot.

If you were to turn left where *Bayview* meets *Muddy Hollow* soon you will reach a gate and the *Muddy Hollow Trailhead*. There are a few spaces for cars.

When you go through the gate and are in the parking area, if you go straight you are on a road that is open to cars. It is a few minutes before you reach the paved Limantour Road. If you cross here it is 0.3 miles to the Youth Hostel. (From the Youth Hostel it is possible to re-connect to either *Laguna* or the *Coast trail* to return to the Five Brooks parking lot).

If you do NOT go straight to the Youth Hostel, but instead go through the gate on the dirt road that dead-ends, very soon on your right you will see the *Estero trail*.

Just before *Estero* if you cross a wooden bridge and go 1.8 miles, this will take you to Limantour Beach (From the beach you can head south on the *Coast Trail* to Coast Camp.)

The *Estero trail* feels like the old west. It is 9.3 miles, 3 feet wide, goes through open space and through trees, and has ocean views. In four miles you will reach *Glenbrook trail (1 DS)*. In another mile is the *Whitegate trail (1 DS)*.

Both *Glenbrook* and *The Whitegate trail* go to *Muddy Hollow Road*. Turn right on *Muddy Hollow* and in two miles you will reach the bottom of *Bucklin Trail*.

If you continue straight on *Estero* past *Whitehead* you will reach *Drakes Head* trail, and this goes west to the ocean. Soon *Estero* will meet with the trail to Sunset Beach, or goes right and will dead end at the Estero parking lot.

STRAIGHT ON INVERNESS RIDGE TRAIL

It takes eight-nine hours from the Five Brooks parking lot round trip to Mt. Vision on a horse. *Inverness Ridge* is six miles long. From the *Bayview* Parking lot it is 2.6 miles to the *Bucklin trail* and 3.8 miles to Mt.Vision.

Going straight on *Inverness Ridge* from the parking lot it is a wide trail with open space and some ocean views.

You will see Tomales Bay on your right. The trail goes up and down and it ends at a paved road. Keep going straight toward the residential area and keep your eyes open for a narrow trail on your left. Take this left.

You are still on *Inverness Ridge trail*. It is now a narrow dirt trail in the woods that is initially steep but then levels out. You will see a government building on your left.

Continuing straight on *Inverness Ridge* and you will arrive at the eastern entrance of the *Bucklin trail*. If you do NOT turn left on *Bucklin* and instead continue straight it is a mile to Mt.Vision.

Bucklin is 1.3 miles from the intersection where *Drakes View* goes left off of *Inverness Ridge*. If you turn left on *Drakes View* it is 1.8 miles long and it intersects with the *Bayview trail*.

(A nice loop if you are on a horse is to turn left on *Bucklin* and back to the Bayview lot, then head back to the Five Brooks parking lot via the *Sky trail, Horse Trail* and *Rift Zone.*)

Turning left on *Bucklin trail* and very soon you will see a bench with a great ocean view. This is a wonderful place to eat lunch. It is 2.2 miles to *Muddy Hollow*, 3.5 miles to the *Glenbrook trail* and 4.2 miles to *Estero trail*.

As you descend westward on *Bucklin* the trail is 3 feet wide. There are some level spots, hills and you will go through a pine forest and see some great ocean views. *Bucklin* ends at Muddy Hollow Road.

Turning Left from *Bucklin* on to Muddy Hollow road can take you back to the Bayview Parking lot (your first left hand turn). Turning right at the bottom of the *Bucklin trail* takes you to the *Estero* and *Glenbrook trails*. *Muddy Hollow trail* will descend and cross over Glenbrook creek, then climbs and meets the *Glenbrook* trail.

Glenbrook is 2.6 miles is level and is not maintained so it can be overgrown in late spring and summer. It ends at a junction with the *Estero trail (difficulty scale 2)*.

Go up the *Estero trail* and it is fifteen miles to the Estero parking lot. You might hear sea lions or see Tule elk. The *Estero trails* descents gently, passes a few eucalyptus trees, then turns and crosses the Glenbrook creek watershed on a bridge. You will see pastureland and ocean views.

If you want to trailer your horse to the Estero trailhead or drive there for a hike, turn left on Sir Francis Drake, go through Inverness Park and drive 8.5 miles. You will see the turnoff on your left.

MT. VISION

If you continue straight on *Inverness Ridge* and in one mile after the turnoff to the *Bucklin trail* there is a gate. *Mt. Vision road* is a challenging horse ride has some incredibly beautiful views in a series of switchbacks climbing to 1,282 feet over 4 miles. There are breathtaking panoramic views of Pt. Reyes, the ocean, meadows, and waterways that comprise Drakes Estero. There are cyclists on this trail.

COAST CAMP

There are several ways to get to *Coast Camp* and back to the Five Brooks parking lot.

You can take *Rift Zone Trail* to Bear Valley Road. Turn left on *Bear Valley Road* to the *Coast Trail* and turn right to *Coast Camp*.

You can also take *Rift Zone Trail* to Bear Valley Road, and go straight past the Morgan Horse ranch and climb up *Horse Trail*. At the top is *Sky Trail* go left about four miles to the *Coast Trail*. Turn right and it is four miles to *Coast Camp*.

It's about 7 miles from the western end of Bear Valley road to Coast Camp.

(On *Bear Valley Road* heading to the *Coast Trail* you will see *Meadow, Old Pine and Baldy* Trails on your right that go up to *the Sky Trail*. Once you arrive at the *Coast trail* turn right/north).

Exiting *Sky trail* and turning right on *Coast trail* you will cross four bridges before you arrive at *Coast Camp*. Where the *Coast Trail* begins to *Coast Camp* is 5.8 miles. On your right you will pass the entrance to *Sky trail* and *Woodward Valley trail*. Sculptured Beach will be on your left.

Another way to *Coast Camp* is to go up *Horse trail* and go left on *Firelane Trail* to the *Coast trail*, and then turn right.

You can also go down *Glen trail* from *Glen Camp* or take the hill from *Millers Point* to *Arch Rock*, where *Bear Valley Road* and the *Coast trail* intersect.

If you are at *Sky Camp* you can head west to the *Sky trail* and turn right and take the *Woodward Valley trail* (a 3 on the difficulty scale) to get to the *Coast trail*. You then turn right on the *Coast trail* to get to *Coast Camp*.

Once you reach *Coast Camp Limantour beach* is another two miles.

This part of the *Coast trail* is mainly level and parallels the ocean with beautiful views. On a horse leaving from *Stewarts Camp*, it is six to eight hours round trip to *Coast Camp*. If you trailer to Bear Valley parking lot it is two hours less.

Coast Camp has a few picnic tables, bathrooms, a horse hitch and a fresh water creek. There's a short narrow trail that goes to the beach.
You can return to Five Brooks Parking lot through the *Rift Zone Trail* or *Millers Point/Glen Camp*.

From MILLERS POINT AND GLEN CAMP TO THE NORTHERN TRAILS

In the chapter on the western trails I described how you get from Five Brooks parking lot to *Millers Point* and *Glen Camp*. At *Glen Camp* you take the *Glen loop trail*. It can take between forty- five minutes to an hour to get from *Glen Camp* to *Bear Valley Road*. Glen Loop is shady and declines. After you leave Glen Camp the trail forks. Go right because left will take you to *Glen Spur North* near *Millers Point*.)

Once you reach *Bear Valley Road* if you go left it can take forty- five minutes to get to *Arch Rock* and the *Coast trail*.

When you reach *Bear Valley Road* **from** *Glen Camp* go straight ahead and across a little bridge to take *Baldy Trail* that goes to *Sky trail*.

It is a steep one-mile climb through Birch and Pine trees. At the top are lovely ocean views. When you reach the *Sky trail* if you go left it goes to the Coast. If you turn right on the *Sky Trail* from *Baldy* in **3** miles is *Sky Camp*.

Traveling east toward *Sky Camp* it becomes more open and there are fewer trees. The trail has mild climbs and declines.

The first trail you will pass is *Old Pine* on your right and declines to *Bear Valley* (closed to horses on weekends).

If you continue west on *Sky trail* you will suddenly be in very tall pines. Continuing east toward *Sky Camp* and you pass the *Woodward Valley trail.* This trail goes west and is two very winding miles to the *Coast trail*. You will be pretty close to *Coast Camp*.

If you go east on the *Sky trail* past *Woodward Valley* you will reach Mt. Wittenberg and *Meadow trail* on your right. (Meadow trail is closed weekends to equestrians. I would suggest walking in front of your horse on parts of *Meadow trail* as it is steep, narrow and there are exposed roots.) Veering left on *Sky trail* instead of going right at the *Meadow trail* takes you to *Sky Camp* in ten to twenty minutes.

(To return to the Five Brooks parking lot from where *Baldy Trail* meets the *Sky* trail go right/east on *Sky Trail* to *Meadow or Horse Trail*. On *Bear Valley Road* turn left toward *Rift Zone*.)

Once you are at *Sky Camp* you have several options. You can reverse your steps back to *Baldy* and then go to *Glen Camp*. Where *Sky trail* meets *Baldy trail* it is 2.4 miles to *Glen Camp*. You could continue for a much longer trip on the *Firelane trail*, or you can take *Horse trail* down to *Rift Zone* and back to the Five Brooks parking lot.

If you want to take Sky Camp back to Five Brooks, you could take the *Sky trail* to Mt. Wittenberg, turn left on *Z Ranch* then right on *Wittenberg or Meadow Trail* down to *Bear Valley Road*. Go left and just before the Visitor Center parking lot turn right on the *Rift Zone* trail.

SUNSET BEACH
Difficulty Scale 2

Driving west on Sir Francis Drake when you reach Olema you turn right. In a few miles you turn left and drive through Inverness till the road forks. Straight is Pierce Point and you turn left. After four miles you will see a sign "Estero Trail". Turn left the go into the parking lot.

You will see the trail from the parking lot. About a half mile from the parking lot you will cross a bridge.

If the tide is low you will walk through some mud so wear good boots. You will encounter a few hills on the trail, and you will enjoy nice views.

It is 2.5 miles to a junction that goes up to *Whitehead trail* and another section of the *Estero trail*. Continue straight 1.5 miles to Sunset beach. Bikes are allowed.

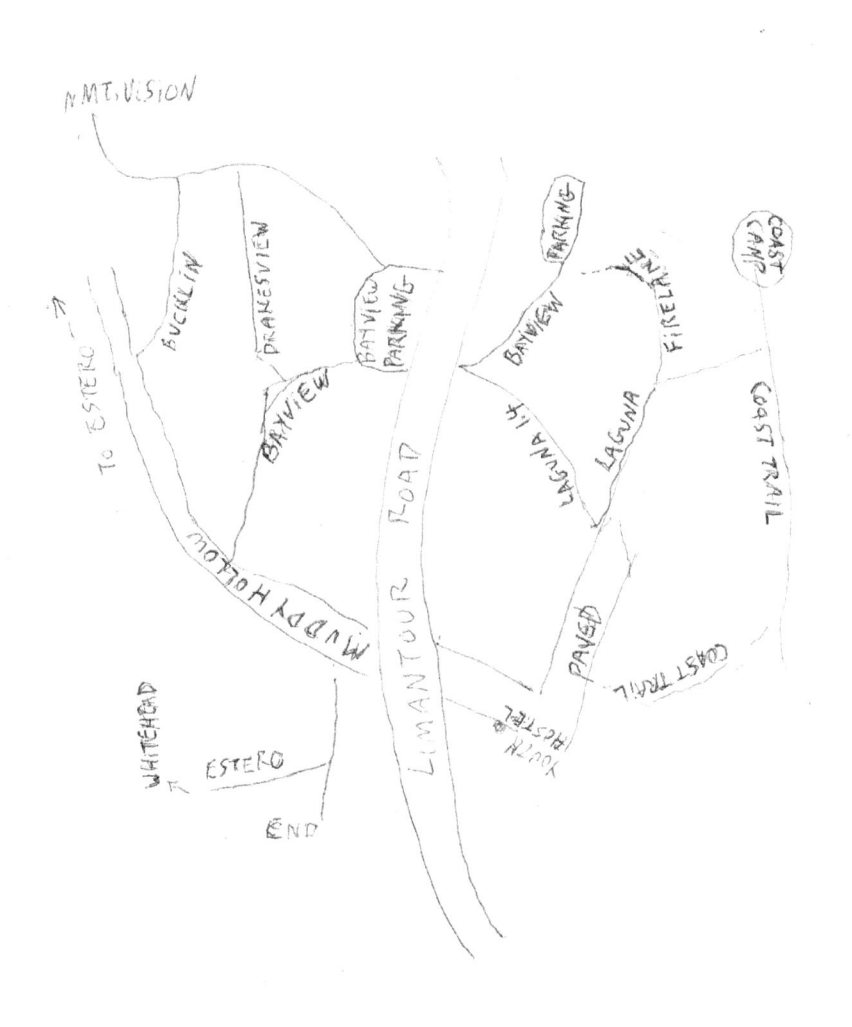

CHAPTER THREE
SOUTH

THE FIVE BROOKS PARKING LOT VIA OLEMA VALLEY TRAIL

From the trailhead parking lot you go past the lake, to *Stewarts trail* and take a left. Very soon you will turn right on *Olema Valley trail*. From Stewarts Camp you go to the main trail and turn left toward the stables. Soon after you pass the road that goes to the parking lot which is on your left take on right on the next (right) trail.

You will be on a level narrow wooded trail and in a quarter of a mile you will go over a bridge. The trail then gets steep for about fifteen minutes than levels out.

In another half mile there's a fork in the trail. (If you go right you are going west up the *Bolema trail,* and *Bolema* is a 3 on the difficulty scale). Go straight on *Olema Valley* trail south toward the town of Bolinas.

A half a mile after the fork the trail will widen, and soon you will have a view of open country. You continue downward and at the bottom the *Randall trail* goes left/east toward Highway One. Stay right on the wider *Olema Valley trail* instead of turning left on *Randal (Randall* begins level and across the Highway become very steep*)*.

Where the *Olema Trail* begins near Five Brooks I would rate it a 3 on the difficulty scale. Once you pass *Bolema* it becomes a 1. *Olema* will become narrow with some ups and downs and poison oak branches may stick out.

In about two miles you will cross a shallow creek, and you will see a private property sign on your left. Don't worry-you are not on private property. There is a house on your left right after you go through the creek.

A mile later the trail ends at Highway One. You could cross the Highway but be careful. The *McGurdy trail* (a 2 on the difficulty scale) climbs 1.7 miles eastward to the *Bolinas Ridge* trail.

The *Texierra trail* (a 3 on the difficulty scale) is about a quarter of a mile after the creek. You will see it on your right. There is a sign that says DOGTOWN and MCGURDY trail 0.4 miles. Turn right up *Texierra* (westward) is a steep wooded trail that's about two miles.

After a mile and a half up you will see a narrow level trail that goes to your left called *Pablo Point*. Watch for poison oak and branches crossing the trail. It takes about half hour to get to the end. It's a quiet magical forest. Rumor has it that a mountain lion lives there so I make lots of noise as I approach the end.

If you continue up *Texierra* and you don't detour to *Pablo Point*, pretty soon you will hit the *Ridge trail.*
If you go left on *Ridge* it's an hour to the *Palomarin trail* - the *Coast trail (3.4 miles)*. This section of *Palomarin* that intersects with *Ridge* can be very rocky and hard on your horse's feet.

Turning right on *Ridge* from *Texierra* in two miles you will reach the intersection where the *Bolema tra*il is right and *Lake Ranch* is left.

When you are at the top of *Texierra* and you turn right toward *Ridge*, if you take another right ON *Ridge* you will reach the intersection of *Bolema* and *Lake ranch* trails. Right on *Bolema* descends to *Olema Valley trail*. Making a left on *Olema Valley* takes you to the Five Brooks parking lot.

Olema Valley to *Texierra* to *Ridge* then *Bolema* takes four hours round trip on a horse.

Once you reach the top of *Texierra* turning left takes you west to *Palomarin*. Right at *Palomarin* becomes the *Coast Trail*, and this section of the *Coast trail* is rocky, has beautiful views and can get crowded with hikers on the weekends. You will be heading north toward Bass Lake, Wildcat Beach and the *Lake Ranch Trail.*

CHAPTER FOUR   EAST

The *Bolinas-Ridge trail* is an eleven- mile long trail. It is a 1 on the difficulty scale. It is wide, in the woods and has open pastures with great views. In the summer there are several cyclists and it can get hot.

There are two ways to get to *Bolinas-Ridge trail* and all of them involve crossing Highway One.

One way to get to *Bolinas Ridge* is to go north from the Five Brooks lot and take the *Rift Zone trail* to the Vedanta Ranch driveway. Turn right then go left for five minutes on the Highway. You will be in the town of Olema and there are steps to climb across the street to the right of the stores. It's then a steep climb of about a mile. You will not be on a formal trail but it will lead to the *Bolinas-Ridge trail*.

The other option is to follow *Olema Valley* south then head East on the *Randall trail* and across Highway One.

THE MCGURDY TRAIL

If you follow the *Olema Valley trail* south and go past *Texierra*, soon you will reach Highway One. It will take you between one and a half to two hours from the Five Brooks Parking Lot to this point, depending if you are hiking or riding. After you pass *Texierra trail* you will go over a small creek. When you cross the Highway there are some large boulders at the entrance to the trail. Be careful that your horse doesn't get scared when she sees the boulders, as you will be watching for cars.

When you enter the trail you head left. There is a sign that reads 1.7 miles to *Bolinas Ridge trail*. You will have a gradual climb on open fields and nice views. The trail will become narrow and you will be in a Pine forest. That won't last too long. You will have open views again and the ground may get rocky and hard. The trail exits at *Bolinas Ridge*.

RANDALL TRAIL TO BOLINAS-RIDGE

You take the *Olema Valley trail* from Five Brooks and head south to the Randall trail (twenty minutes after passing the *Bolema trail* on your right). Turn left onto a narrow trail called *Randall* and soon you will cross a bridge. Soon after is Highway One.

Crossing the Highway on a horse can be dangerous. You should be fine if you are an experienced rider and confident about your horse. Once you cross Highway One you go through a gate. (In nice weather there can be a lot of motorcycles on the weekends). Once you get through the gate there is a steep climb to the top. At the top is s the *Bolinas-Ridge trail*.

BOLINAS RIDGE TRAIL

Bolinas Ridge goes north and south. You can access it by car from the town of Olema on Sir Francis Drake Road, a half mile up the hill facing Fairfax.

The trail is five miles long and is wide and mainly flat. It is open to cyclists, hikers and equestrians. The southern end is up the hill from Dogtown. If you begin from Sir Francis Drake you will have open space with views, and the remainder of the trail then is in the woods.

Once on the trail you can branch out left to get to Sam Taylor Park. The *Randall* and *McGurdy* trails descend off to the right toward Highway One.

On the weekends in nice weather there are often several bicyclists. The open space areas can be quite hot in the summer.

At the top of *Randall* you are about half way between the southern and northern points. From the top of *Randall* you can go right on *Bolinas Ridge* to the *McGurdy trail*. Descending down the *McGurdy* trail you can then cross Highway One and take *Olema Valley trail* back to the Five Brooks Parking lot.

At the top of Randall if you turn left (north) on Bolinas ridge there are some nice views on your left and large pine trees on your right.

After about a half-mile you will see a small sign that says "to Jewel 4.8". (This refers to the *Jewel trail*, a 2 on the difficulty scale that connects with Sam Taylor Park.)

On your right a sign reads "Shafter's Bridge 1.7".

If you go right this trail is a steep descent to Shafter's Bridge in Samuel Taylor Park. The return is a steep uphill but there is a water trough for horses half way down.

59

Once you reach the bottom you will see Sir Francis Drake Road. If you cross it you will see a narrow bridge. BE CAREFUL CROSSING THIS ROAD. After you cross the bridge you go left on a wide trail. This is part of Sam Taylor Park. Fifteen minutes later there is a steep trail on your right that will take you to Mt. Barnabe. At the very end there is a hostile resident living in private home. The views are great at the top. If you are riding your horse to Mt. Barnabe and back, plan on it being an eight-ten hour trip.

If you head back to the *Bolinas Ridge trail* from Shafters Bridge, once you reach *Bolinas Ridge* you have a few options.

Turning right (north) in a quarter of a mile you will have to go through a gate. You will see a lot of open space and can head toward *Jewel trail*. *Jewel* descends a mile down to the back part of Sam Taylor Park.

On your way to *Jewel* there is a way to return to Five Brooks by going down to the steps in the town of Olema, but it is a steep decline and easy to get lost. If you could find the left turn when you are heading toward *Jewel*, there is no formal trail and it's a matter of following the power lines.

If you can find your way to the Olema steps you then have to cross Sir Francis Drake Road and go left five hundred yards on Rt. One. Then take a right on the Vedanta Retreat driveway. In about ten minutes you would take a left hand turn through the cow pasture (a gate) and continuing straight end up on the *Rift Zone trail*.

Unless you know the area well I recommend coming back to the Five brooks parking lot by retracing your steps on *Bolinas Ridge*, turning right down the *Randall trail*, crossing the Highway, and turning right on *Olema Valley trail*.

Legal trails for cyclists:
(ten to a group maximum)

Randall, McGurdy, Bolinas Ridge, Bear Valley Road, The Coast trail from the northern trailhead near the Hostel to Coast camp,, Stewarts trail, Olema Valley trail, Sky trail from Limantour Road to Sky Camp, Glen trail, Inverness ridge, and the Estero trail from the Sir Francis Drake road trailhead to Whitegate trail.

<u>Camping</u>: Reservations may be made online at **Recreation.gov**. Reservations may also be made by phone by calling toll free 877-444-6777

WATERING TROUGHS FOR HORSES

BEAR VALLEY VISITORS CENTER
WILDCAT CAMP SKY CAMP
RIFT ZONE (cow pasture)
The trail to Shafter's bridge from Bolinas Ridge

GLOSSERY

TRAIL   PAGES

ALAMEA 9, 10, 12, 16, 20

ARCH ROCK 30, 31, 38, 47, 48

BALDY 30, 33, 36, 37, 38, 47, 48, 50

BASS LAKE 6, 12, 16, 18, 19, 55

BAYVIEW 39, 40, 41, 42, 43, 44, 45

BEAR VALLEY ROAD 13, 21, 24, 29, 30, 31, 33, 36, 37, 38, 46, 47, 48, 50, 51

BOLEMA 3, 4, 5, 6, 9, 10, 11, 15 16, 20, 24, 37, 53, 54, 55, 57

BOLINAS RIDGE 54, 56, 57, 58, 59, 60

BUCKLIN 42, 43, 44, 45, 46

COAST CAMP 30, 37, 38, 39, 40, 41, 43, 46, 47

COAST TRAIL 4, 5, 6, 7, 10, 12, 13, 15, 16, 17, 18, 19, 21, 22, 24, 30, 37-41, 43, 46, 47. 48, 50, 55

COAST GLEN SPUR SOUTH & NORTH 24, 48

CRYSTAL LAKE 6

DRAKES VIEW 44

DRAKESHEAD 43

ENVIRONMENTAL CENTER   41
ESTERO 42-45, 51
FIR TOP 8, 9
FIRELANE 38, 39, 40, 41, 47, 50
GLEN CAMP 7-10, 13, 21-24, 29, 30, 37, 47, 48, 50
GLEN TRAIL 7-10, 13, 22, 23, 24, 30, 36, 37, 47
GREENPICKER 7-13, 20, 23, 24, 36
GLENBROOK   42, 44, 45
HIDDEN VALLEY   40
HORSETRAIL 31, 33, 36, 38, 39, 44, 46, 47, 50
INVERNESS RIDGE 43, 44, 46, 62
JEWEL 59, 60
KULE LOKO   31, 32
LAGUNA 38-42
LAKE RANCH 4, 5, 6, 9, 11, 12, 15-18, 55
LIMANTOUR RD. & BEACH 30, 37, 38, 40-43, 47
MCGURDY 54, 57, 58, 59, 62
MEADOW   30, 33, 36, 47, 50, 51
MILLERS POINT 10, 13, 21-24, 31, 37, 47, 48
MORGAN RANCH 29, 31, 32
Mt. BARNABE 60
MT. WITTENBERG and trail 30, 36, 37

MT. VISION 43, 46

MUDD LAKE 6

MUDDY HOLLOW ROAD 39, 41-45

OLEMA VALLEY 3, 5, 6, 16, 24, 53, 55, 56, 57, 61

OLEMA MARSH 31, 32, 33

OLD PINE 30, 33, 38, 47

OLD OUT 4, 6, 7, 9, 12, 16, 17, 20

OCEAN LAKE LOOP 17

PABLO POINT 54, 55

PALOMARIN 4, 5, 11, 16, 18, 55

PELICAN LAKE

RANDAL 53, 56, 57, 58, 59, 61, 62

NARROW RIDGE TRAIL 4, 7, 9, 11, 12, 16, 20, 24

WIDER RIDGE 5, 7, 9, 12, 16, 24, 37, ?

RIFT ZONE 27, 28, 30, 31, 33, 36, 44, 48, 50, 51, 56, 61, 62

SCULPTURED BEACH 30

SHAFTERS BRIDGE 60

SKY CAMP 30, 31, 32, 33, 36, 37, 38, 39, 41, 47, 49, 50, 51

SKY TRAIL 30, 33, 36 -38, 41, 44, 46, 47, 48, 50, 51

STEWARTS TRAIL 3-11, 14, 15, 16, 20, 22, 24, 27, 36, 53, 62

STEWART'S CAMP 4, 5, 20, 23, 27, 47, 53

SUNSET BEACH   43, 51

TEXIERRA 4, 5, 11, 54, 55, 57

WITTENBERG TRAIL 30

WHITEGATE 43

WILDCAT CAMP **and** BEACH 6, 7, 9, 12, 13, 15-19, 24, 55, 62

WOODWARD VALLEY 37, 47, 50

YOUTH HOSTEL 38, 39, 40, 42

Z-RANCH   31, 33, 36, 39, 51

Birds at Point Reyes National Seashore

Pelicans, Cormorants, Herons, Bitterns, & Egrets, Storks, Ducks, Geese, Swans, New World Vultures, Hawks, Kites, Eagles, Falcons, New World Quail, Rails, Gallinules, Coots, Cranes, Oystercatcher, Sandpipers, Gulls, Terns, Skimmers, Auks, Pigeons, Doves, Owls, blue jays, Hummingbirds, Kingfishers, Woodpeckers, Larks, Swallows, Crows, Chickadees, Titmice, Bushtits, Nuthatches, Wrens, Dippers, Kinglets, Old World Warblers, Gnatcatchers, Thrushes, Babblers, Mockingbirds, Thrashers, Pipits, Cardinals, and Finches.

BASS LAKE

PELICAN LAKE

Poison Oak Usually green or red leaves

Flowering Plants of Point Reyes National Seashore

Aceraceae (Maple Famly)

Agavaceae (Agave Family)

Aizoaceae (Fig-marigold Family)

Alismataceae (Water-plantain Family)

Amaranthaceae (Amaranth Family)

Anacardiaceae (Sumac Family)

Apiaceae (Carrot Family)

Apocynaceae (Dogbane Family)

Aquifoliaceae (Holly Family)

Euphorbiaceae (Spurge Family)

Fabaceae (Legume Family)

Fagaceae (Oak Family)

Frankeniaceae (Frankenia Family)

Garryaceae (Silk Tassel Family)

Gentianaceae (Gentian Family)

Geraniaceae (Geranium Family)

Grossulariaceae (Gooseberry Family)

Gunneraceae (Gunnera Family)

Haloragaceae (Water-milfoil Family)

Hippocastanaceae (Buckeye Family)

Hydrophyllacea (Waterleaf Family)

Hypericaceae (St. John's Wort Family)

Iridaceae (Iris Family)

Papaveraceae (Poppy Family)

Philadelphaceae (Mockorange Family)

Pittosporaceae (Pittosporum Family)

Plantaginaceae (Plantain Family)

Platanaceae (Sycamore Family)

Plumbaginaceae (Leadwort Family)

Poaceae (Grass Family)

Polemoniaceae (Phlox Family)

Polygalaceae (Milkwort Family)

Polygonaceae ((Buckwheat Family)

Polypodiaceae (Polypod Family)

Portulacaceae (Purslane Family)

Potamogetonaceae (Pondweed Family)

Primulaceae (Primrose Family)

Ranunculaceae (Buttercup Family)

Rhamnaceae (Buckthorn Family)

Rosaceae (Rose Family)

Araceae (Arum Family)

Araliaceae (Ginseng Family)

Aristolochiaceae (Pipevine Family)

Asteraceae (Sunflower Family)

Berberidaceae (Barberry Family)

Betulaceae (Birch Family)

Boraginaceae (Borage Family)

Brassicaceae (Mustard Family)

Callitrichaceae (Water-starwort Family)

Campanulaceae (Bellflower Family)

Cannabaceae (Hemp Family)

Caprifoliaceae (Honeysuckle Family)

Caryophyllaceae (Pink Family)

Celastraceae (Staff-tree Family)

Ceratophyllaceae (Hornwort Family)

Chenopodiaceae (Goosefoot Family)

Cistaceae (Rock-rose Family)

Convolvulaceae (Morning Glory Family)

Cornaceae (Dogwood Family)

Crassulaceae (Stonecrop Family)

Cucurbitaceae (Gourd Family)

Cuscutaceae (Dodder Family)

Cyperaceae (Sedge Family)

Dipsacaceae (Teasel Family)

Ericaceae (Heather Family)

Juncaceae (Rush Family)

Juncaginaceae (Arrow-grass Family)

Lamiaceae (Mint Family)

Lauraceae (Laurel Family)

Lemnaceae (Duckweed Family)

Liliaceae (Lily Family)

Limnanthaceae (Meadowfoam Family)

Linaceae (Flax Family)

Lythraceae (Loosestrife Family)

Malvaceae (Mallow Family)

Myricaceae (Wax Myrtle Family)

Myrtaceae (Myrtle Family)

Nyctaginaceae (Four O'clock Family)

Nymphaeaceae (Waterlily Family)

Oleaceae (Olive Family)

Onagraceae (Evening-primrose Family)

Ophioglossaceae (Adder's-tongue Family)

Orchidaceae (Orchid Family)

Orobanchaceae (Broom-rape Family)

Oxalidaceae (Oxalis Family)

Rubiaceae (Madder Family)

Rutaceae (Rue Family)

Salicaceae (Willow Family)

   Saxifrage Family

Scrophylariaceae (Figwort Family)

Solanaceae (Nightshade Family)

Thymelaaeceae (Mezereum Family)

Tropaeolaceae (Nasturtium Family)

Typhaceae (Cattail Family)

Urticaceae (Nettle Family)

Valerianaceae (Valerian Family)

Malvaceae (Mallow Family)

Myricaceae (Wax Myrtle Family)

Myrtaceae (Myrtle Family)

Nyctaginaceae (Four O'clock Family)

Nymphaeaceae (Waterlily Family)

Oleaceae (Olive Family)

Onagraceae (Evening-primrose Family)

Ophioglossaceae (Adder's-tongue Family)

Orchidaceae (Orchid Family)

Orobanchaceae (Broom-rape Family)

Oxalidaceae (Oxalis Family)

Rubiaceae (Madder Family)

Rutaceae (Rue Family)

Salicaceae (Willow Family)

Valerianaceae (Valerian Family)

Verbenaceae (Vervain Family)

Violaceae (Violet Family)

Viscaceae (Mistletoe Family)

Zosteraceae (Eel-grass Family)

Cone-bearing Plants (Gymnosperms) of Point Reyes National Seashore

*** indicates non-native species

Family Cupressaceae (**Cypress Family**)
Calocedrus decurrens -Incense Cedar ***
Cupressus glabra - Southern Arizona Cypress ***
Cupressus macrocarpa- Monterey Cypress ***
Cupressus sargentii- Sargent Cypress ***
Juniperus sp.- Juniper ***

Pinaceae (**Pine Family**)
Pinus contorta ssp. Contorta- Shore Pine
Pinus muricata-*** Bishop Pine
Pinus radiate- Monterey Pine ***
Pseudotsuga menziesii var. menziesii- Douglas-fir

Taxaceae (**Yew Family**) Taxus brevifolia- Western Yew
Taxodiaceae (**Bald Cypress Family**)
Sequoia sempervirens- Redwood

Fern & Fern Allies of Point Reyes National Seashore

Mosquito Fern

Deer Fern

Chain Fern

Coastal Lady Fern

Coastal Wood Fern

Spreading Wood Fern

Western Sword Fern

Common Horsetail

Common Scouring Rush

Giant Horsetail

Quillwort

Seep Quillwort

Leathery Grapefern

American pillwort

Leather Fern

Five-finger fern

California Maiden-hair

Goldenback Fern

Spike-moss

COYOTE

BOBCAT **ELK**

The tule elk herds had virtually disappeared by 1860, thirteen years before the state awarded them complete protection. In the spring of 1978, two bulls and eight cows were brought in from the San Luis Island Wildlife Refuge near Los Banos. The elk were contained within a temporary three acre enclosure to allow for adjustment to their new surroundings. That summer, six of the cows bore calves. In the fall, seventeen elk were released from the enclosure on Tomales Point to 1,050 hectares (2,600 acres) of open grassland and coastal scrub. By the summer of 1988, the population was at ninety-three animals. The population census taken in 2000 counted over 400 elk. In 2009, over 440 were counted at Tomales Point, making the Point Reyes herds one of the largest populations in California.

The tule elk can be found in several locations within the park but the best chance of seeing them is in the Tule Elk Preserve at Tomales Point. They graze freely and are often seen near the road as you drive into the preserve.

- For your own safety, always observe elk from a distance.
- Use binoculars and spotting scopes. If an elk becomes alert or nervous and begins to move away, you are too close.
- If viewing from your car, pull off the road or park in designated areas.
- If you are on foot, stay on the trail; do not come between a cow and calf, a bull and a group of cows, or two bulls challenging each other.
- Watch quietly; whisper. Move slowly.
- Do not feed the elk. Feeding elk or any other wildlife is unhealthy for the animals, potentially dangerous for visitors, and strictly prohibited.
- Ride your bicycle only on designated trails. Within the Tomales Point Tule Elk Reserve, bicycles are only permitted on the Pierce Point Road. Bicycles are prohibited on the Tomales Point and McClures Beach trails.
- Pets are prohibited in most areas where elk may be seen, including the Tomales Point Tule Elk Reserve.
- Do not collect or remove elk antlers. They are an important source of calcium for many wildlife species such as rodents and deer.

A brief history of Point Reyes National Seashore

Long before Point Reyes became a National Seashore it was home to the Coast Miwok tribes. Living on the Point Reyes peninsula for centuries, the Coast Miwok found their lives uprooted when they were relocated to nearby Missions in the late 1700s to early 1800s. After the Coast Miwoks' expulsion, Mexican rancheros grazed cattle on the land during the 1830s. When California became part of the United States in 1850 the land was divided into 32 tenant-run diaries and cattle ranches to keep up with the demand from the urban centers of the San Francisco Bay.

World War II even brought mining and military installations to this future "untrammeled" wilderness area. A great deal of the current contention lies around the fundamental issue of working landscapes as parkland. While it may be controversial, the presence of grazing on the land at Point Reyes National Seashore has provided a number of ecological benefits, such as a greater number and variety of native grasses as compared to areas that have suffered shrub invasion where grazing was removed.

After studying the area since the 1930s as a potential location for a public recreational area to serve the residents of the growing city of San Francisco, in 1962 in an attempt to stave off a potential housing development, the National Park Service decided to establish the Point Reyes National Seashore (PRNS) as a 53,000 acre recreational area, including a 21,000 acre pastoral zone, located on the Point Reyes Peninsula in Marin County, California.

In 1976 an additional 25,370 acres were designated as the Phillip Burton Wilderness Area at Point Reyes National Seashore. Today PRNS is a 71,028 acre park preserve, and has continued to be an area of mixed use between commercial and recreational activities, allowing for some agricultural uses to continue on the protected lands.

In recent years there have been a number of issues at Point Reyes that have escalated controversy and caused a fracturing between the tenants at Point Reyes National Seashore, the National Park Service, park visitors and environmental groups. Some of the recent issues causing tension include the removal of Drakes Bay Oyster Company from the park, ranchers being denied renewal of their leases at the seashore, Tule elk competing with ranchers' cattle herds, and an outdated general management plan.

However, despite the disputes over the landscape that have been building in the last few years, the parties all agree that Point Reyes is unique place worthy of protection.

Point Reyes National Seashore is a thriving mixture of agriculture and parkland. An experiment of sorts between a combination of private and public uses in order to please the multiple stakeholders. The 1964 Wilderness Act, that was used to establish the Phillip Burton Wilderness Area at Point Reyes National Seashore in 1976, envisioned wilderness as an, "…area where the earth and its community of life are untrammeled by man, where man himself is a visitor who does not remain…without permanent improvements or human habitation, which is protected and managed so as to preserve its natural conditions.

While this was the vision of wilderness seen through the eyes of Wilderness Society's Howard Zahniser, the author of the Act, the Act also contained many exceptions, such as non-conforming prior uses. Point Reyes never quite fit the ideal model of a wilderness area, as it was the first area to receive the designation of potential wilderness lands. While the NPS may have a history of accepting alternative uses within the park, it appears with recent tensions and decisions that they are headed down the traditional path of park management, one that excludes people, other than tourists, from their vision.

ABOUT THE AUTHOR

Dennis Portnoy is a psychotherapist in private practice in San Francisco. He also gives presentations and workshops on burnout prevention, self-care and counteracting the stress that comes from being in a helper role.

Made in the USA
Middletown, DE
01 September 2021